Ape's great escape

Russell Punter

Illustrated by David Semple

Ape's in chains for stealing grapes.

But he has planned a great escape.

"The guards won't see me flee this jail.
My plan's so grand, it just can't fail."

"This key I made will set me free."

He bends the bars,

then jumps...

Whoopee!

His landing doesn't go to plan.
He falls slap, bang...into a can.

WET PAINT

PAINT

PAINT

But Ape has made a great mistake...

The stones are really dozing crocs!

Ape screams and hollers.

What a shock!

"I've reached the jungle. I'm okay!"

But a steamy swamp lies in the way.

"I'll swing across on this thick vine.
One easy leap and I'll be fine."

Wrong once more, for it's a snake!

His hissing fit makes poor Ape quake.

Soon the mountains are in view.
"I'm nearly home," cheers Ape.

Woo-hoo!

But silly Ape's loud yell of hope...

brings boulders rolling down the slope.

At last Ape makes it to his cave.
"I'm home!" gasps Ape.

"Come out! Come out!"

Ape gives a frown.
The prison guards have
tracked him down!

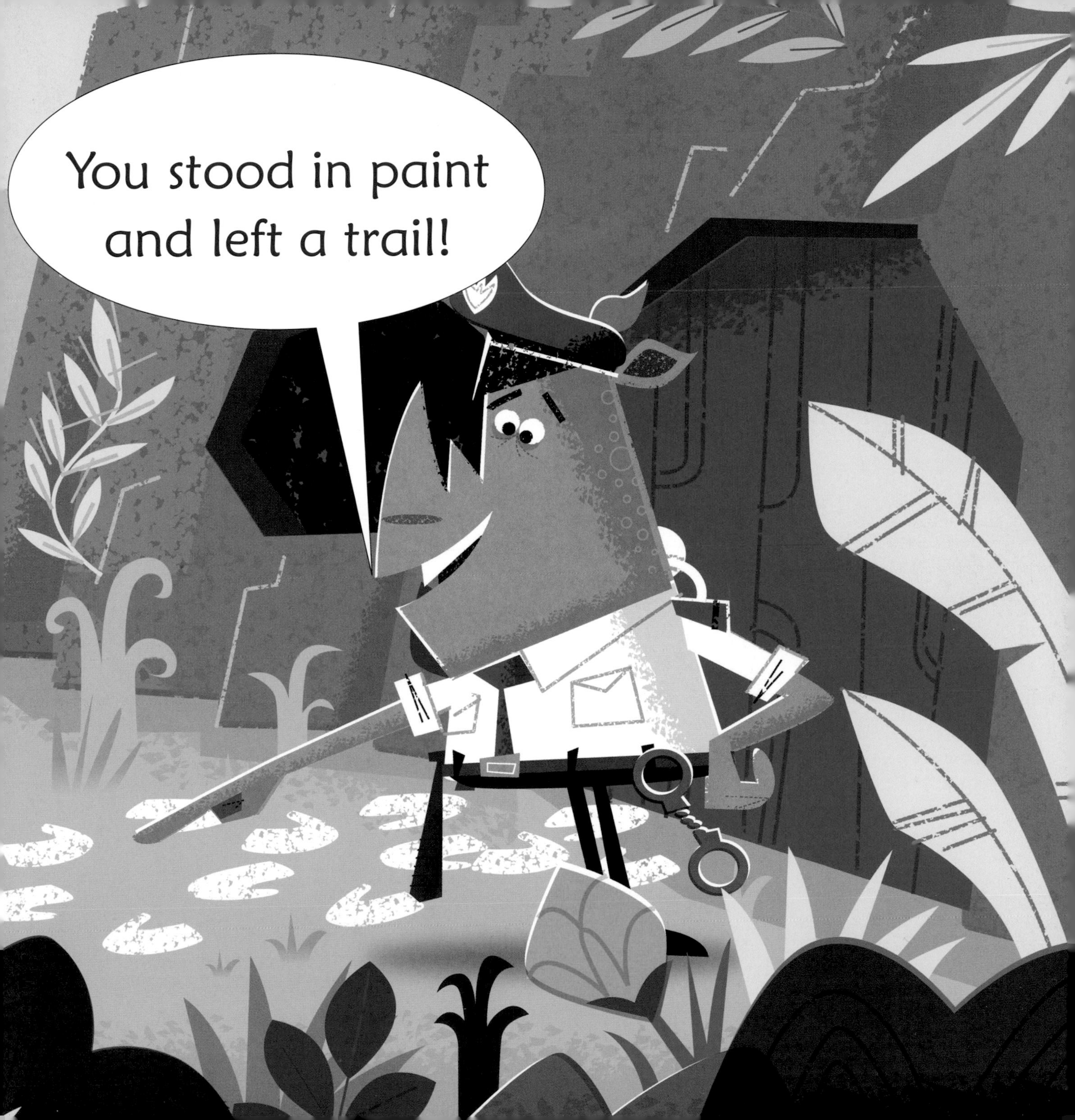
You stood in paint and left a trail!

About phonics

Phonics is a method of teaching reading used extensively in today's schools. At its heart is an emphasis on identifying the *sounds* of letters, or combinations of letters, that are then put together to make words. These sounds are known as phonemes.

Starting to read
Learning to read is an important milestone for any child. The process can begin well before children start to learn letters and put them together to read words. The sooner children can discover books and enjoy stories and language, the better they will be prepared for reading themselves, first with the help of an adult and then independently.

You can find out more about phonics on the Usborne Very First Reading website, **www.usborne.com/veryfirstreading** (US readers go to **www.veryfirstreading.com**). Click on the **Parents** tab at the top of the page, then scroll down and click on **About synthetic phonics**.

Phonemic awareness

An important early stage in pre-reading and early reading is developing phonemic awareness: that is, listening out for the sounds within words. Rhymes, rhyming stories and alliteration are excellent ways of encouraging phonemic awareness.

In this story, your child will soon identify the *a* sound, as in **grape** and **lake**. Look out, too, for rhymes such as **quake** – **snake** and **fail** – **trail**.

Hearing your child read

If your child is reading a story to you, don't rush to correct mistakes, but be ready to prompt or guide if he or she is struggling. Above all, do give plenty of praise and encouragement.

Edited by Jenny Tyler
Designed by Hope Reynolds

Reading consultants: Alison Kelly and Anne Washtell

First published in 2018 by Usborne Publishing Ltd., Usborne House, 83-85 Saffron Hill, London EC1N 8RT, England.
www.usborne.com Copyright © 2018 Usborne Publishing Ltd.